MA

Description

WORK HARD FOR YOU

———————— ● ————————

CRAFTING UNPUTDOWNABLE FICTION

BETH YARNALL

www.BethYarnall.com

Making Description Work Hard For You
Beth Yarnall

Print ISBN: 978-1940811833
Digital ISBN: 978-1940811895

Editor: Laurie Larsen
Cover Design: Humble Nations

MAKING

Description

WORK HARD FOR YOU

———————●———————

CRAFTING UNPUTDOWNABLE FICTION

Foreword

I wrote my first book and immediately sent it out into the world, thinking I'd get nothing but praise back. Yeah, *that* didn't happen. When the comments from contest judges and editors and agents started to come in I was quite taken aback. I wasn't the literary genius I thought I was. But I wanted to learn so I paid attention to the feedback I got and worked hard to shore up my weaknesses.

My very first lesson on description came from a contest judge who was a published author. She pointed out where my description worked hard for me and where it didn't. One of the places she pointed out was the beginning of chapter two. It started with this little gem:

I really liked Rebecca's house, a 1950's California ranch style set into a suburban neighborhood called Lemon Heights. Lemon Heights isn't a real city but an area in the city of Santa Ana, which is tucked away in the center of Orange County California. It's where we grew up. In fact our parents have a house two streets over. It's very upper middle class in a city that is all middle class. Rebecca's house is perched up on top of a gently sloping front yard, perfectly maintained by her husband Michael Schaffer or at least by the gardeners he hired.

I wasted a lot of valuable page real estate describing a house and neighborhood that never appeared in the book again. I made the reader pay attention to unimportant details and it was *boring*, which the contest judge pointed out on my entry:

Try to make this description work harder or cut it if it's not important to the story. What's important about this? What does it tell me about your heroine or her sister that's vital to the story?

The answer was a resounding *nothing*. This description didn't give the reader any information about who my characters are. It just laid there on the page taking up space. At the beginning of chapter two, no less!

The judge's comments caused a light bulb moment for me. They changed my writing and the way I approach description. They also inspired my *Making Description Work Hard For You* workshop, which I've given for writers' groups and conferences. I soon discovered that a one-hour workshop wasn't long enough to show writers everything description can do for them in a story, so I expanded on it and turned it into a book.

This book is my way to pay it forward and honor the judge who changed the way I write description. I hope it inspires you to write description that works hard for you and takes your writing to the next level.

Beth Yarnall

Table of Contents

Introduction

Long, flowing, red hair... check. Violet eyes... check. Chiseled jaw, lock of hair over a prominent brow, broad, muscular shoulders... check, check, check.

Description is often the most under and misused tool in a writer's toolbox. It can be as dry as bone dust or read like a laundry list. But used well, description can pull the reader deeper into the story. Good description should draw the lines of the picture and allow the reader to fill in the color. As Stephen King said, "Description begins in the writer's imagination, but should finish in the reader's."

Use description judiciously and wisely. When you take up a lot of page time describing an object or character, you're telling the reader to pay attention, this is important. If you spend your describing wad on a place or character that only appears in one scene and then never again in the rest of the book you'll confuse your reader. They'll spend the rest of the book wondering why that person or place was important and when it's going to appear again.

Description can be paragraphs long or as short as a sentence, depending on what is happening in the story. Remember you're drawing pictures in your readers' minds. Do you only want to give them a hint of what a character thinks about another character or object or do you want to give them a much broader view? It will be up to you, the author, to decide what your reader should pay attention to and remember and what they shouldn't.

Description is as much about the feeling, person or object being described as it is about the character doing the actual describing. This is deep point of view, bringing the reader into the head and heart of a character. Deep point of view allows the reader to see and feel every aspect of the story through the characters' experiences, thoughts and feelings. Using description to achieve deep point of view is one of the most powerful tools an author can use to create stories and characters readers will remember long after the last page is turned.

Author's Note

In this book I've presented samples from other author's work (with proper credit) as well as my own. Not because I think my writing is special or precious, but because sometimes it was the most expedient way for me to illustrate a particular point. I could talk all day long about how to do something, but sometimes that's not enough. You have to see the principle in action in order to fully take it in.

I hope you enjoy these authors' excerpts as much as I do and will consider reading one or more of their books. Many are award winning and best selling authors. I promise you won't be disappointed.

Filtering Description Through Characters' Experiences

A Character's Past

Characters do not spring from the ground fully formed. Their experiences—their life journeys—shape who they are. Everything that's ever happened to them, they carry with them. Backstory is not only vital to the goal, motivation, and conflict of your characters, it also influences how your characters view their world and the people in it. Their prejudices, desires, opinions, dislikes, likes, ambitions, impressions, and fears will be reflected in the way they describe the people, places, and things they come to know.

Backstory in Description

Their experiences will also color their perception and judgment. This will especially play a part when characters meet. What impressions do they have of the other character? Will they like them or dislike them? Will their initial assessment be accurate or biased based on their backstory or their experience with characters who have the same or similar lifestyle? Will the other character remind them of someone they know or used to know? How will that affect their feelings about that other character?

A woman might be wary of the man she just met based on her experiences with men who look or behave similar to him. Your heroine who has sworn off bad boys due to negative experiences will describe an alpha, tattooed biker much differently than a female character who is excited about the prospect of taking a walk on the wild side.

No two people can ever look at the same person or object and describe it the same way because no two people have the same life experiences. Use that in your work.

Where a Character Is Now

Just as a character's past influences how they see the world, so does their age, sex, occupation, and social standing.

A hairstylist might describe a person by their hairstyle or hair color. A CEO might describe a person by their level of professionalism. A police officer might describe a person by their actions and reactions, making a general note of appearance like they might for a report. An architect might describe a building differently than a layperson. A young couple might look at a house in bad repair and think—fixer-upper. An older couple might look at the same house and think—too much work.

From **Rush** by Beth Yarnall:

He was large—well over six feet tall and as broad as a doublewide.

This is the heroine describing the hero when she sees him for the first time. What information does it give the reader about the heroine? Notice I said *heroine* and not hero? Sure, we get that he's a big guy, but it also gives us a little something about the heroine's background. She didn't describe him as being *as broad as a barn* or *as wide as a mansion gate*. She said *as broad as a doublewide*. This description tips off the reader that the heroine probably lived or is living in a trailer park and that maybe she doesn't come from a lot of money.

From **Rush** by Beth Yarnall:
With his sudden intake of air came the

recognition that this tiny woman could do him more harm than a grenade strapped to his chest.

What information does this description give us about the hero? We get the sense that he cares for her, sure. But what about the use of *do him more harm than a grenade strapped to his chest?* Is this the wording of an accountant or someone who is or has been in the military? If you guessed military, you're right. He's a retired Navy SEAL.

Keep in mind who your character is as well as where they came from when writing description.

Voice

Each of your characters should have their own unique voice. Just as in dialog, each of your characters will have words or phrases they use to describe things that are unique to them. A character who has spent a lot of time on a ship might use nautical terms. A younger character would use current vernacular and be more exclamatory. A character from another country would use words from and make comparisons to his homeland.

Your military hero might curse more than your elderly church-going character. Then again, maybe not. Your character's voice in how they describe their world will be an important part of your story and give the reader more insight to your characters. Remember, the reader always has more information than the characters in the story. One of the ways you will feed it to them is through description. If your character's internal descriptions don't match who they present themselves to be to the other characters in the story, you will create a distinctive character readers can identify with. Giving your characters their own individual voice will deepen the reader's attachment to that character.

Show Don't Tell

You've probably heard of the idiom *show don't tell*, but how does it relate to description?

As Anton Chekhov said, "Don't tell me the moon is shining; show me the glint of light on broken glass."

Showing creates vivid images in your reader's mind. It inserts your reader directly into the scene right along with your character. They'll cry when your character cries and laugh when he laughs.

Telling summarizes what is happening for the reader. It's a statement or synopsis about what is happening to a character in the scene. It creates distance between the reader and the story.

Showing and telling do essentially the same thing—relay information to the reader. But *showing* will draw the reader in, while *telling* creates a buffer. Readers want to *experience* a story, not be *told* about it. Showing requires descriptive words whereas telling is just the facts ma'am. News reporters and nonfiction authors *tell* you what is happening. Movie directors and fiction authors *show* you. *Showing* requires more words than *telling* and is much more illustrative and theatrical.

Having said that, there will be times when you will want to *tell* to move the story along. You can't *show* everything or your book will be a bagillion pages long. There will be times when you'll have to do some judicious *telling* to move the story along. Be mindful and purposeful about it.

Showing vs. telling often comes down to word choice. Get used to me saying this because I'm going to point it out a lot. Word choice matters in description. It can be the difference between a reader throwing your book at the wall or placing it lovingly on their keeper shelf.

Telling Words

Telling words filter the reader's experience rather than drawing them into the story. Words like felt, saw, heard, and thought *tell* the reader what is happening.

An example of telling: Jenny didn't like spiders. She thought they were gross.

Okay, we get that Jenny doesn't like spiders. So what? This passage doesn't make us *feel* Jenny's revulsion. It only *tells* us about it and that's not good enough.

Example of showing:

Spiders had to be the most disgusting creatures. All of those hairy legs skittering about. Anything that moved like that had to be up to no good.

In the second example we're deep into Jenny's point of view—we're in her head, hearing her thoughts as if they are our own. We *picture* a spider moving about in our mind's eye. We *feel* Jenny's revulsion. There's no buffer between Jenny and us. We're fully immersed in her point of view.

Pronouns and Proper Names

If you find yourself using a lot of proper names and pronouns when describing, you're probably using them alongside telling words- *Bob* felt, *Cindy* saw, *they* heard, and so on. As in our previous example with Jenny and her spiders— *Jenny* didn't like spiders. *She* thought they were gross. This separates your reader from your characters and you never want to do that. The closer you can bring your reader to your characters, the better.

Active Verbs vs Passive and Inactive Verbs

Passive and inactive verbs are sneaky. They can creep into your work without you even realizing it. They assist where oftentimes no help is needed.

Keep It Active

Active verbs are the combo meal in description—they're action with a side of adjective. Active verbs do more than show what your character is doing; they describe how your character is doing it. Make sure you're using the most active verbs you can in your description.

He held the baby. vs. He cradled the baby.

Cradled does more than show what he's doing with the baby, it shows how he might feel about the baby.

She went into the house. vs. She stormed into the house.

Stormed gives the reader insight into her emotional state as she enters the house and she's probably not happy.

In these two examples the word choices of *cradled* and *stormed* are doing double duty. They show what is happening and give insight into the character's feelings. Whenever possible choose verbs that will do more for you.

Passive and Inactive Verbs

If you find yourself putting words such as is, are, am, was, were, be, being, been, do, does, did, has, have, had, might, or may before verbs—you're using *passive verbs* or passive voice.

Example of passive: Becky was going to the store.

Was about to... maybe she will, maybe she won't. We don't know and likely we don't care.

The excessive use of passive verbs is the most telling sign of a beginning writer. Overusing passive verbs is flat out lazy writing. Don't cheat yourself and don't cheat your reader. Before turning your manuscript in to your editor or agent or entering it in a contest, do a final round editing pass to look for passive verbs and weed them out wherever you can.

Inactive verbs such as started to, began to, proceeded to, could, would, there was, there are, there is, there were, seemed to, tried to— dilute the verb you're using.

Example of inactive: Becky started to go to the store.

She *started* to go, but we don't really know if she went or not. Be sure this ambiguity is what you want to convey before using inactive verbs. A good example of when you'd want to use an inactive verb is: Becky started to go to the store, but Julie called her back.

Example of active: Becky went to the store.

She went... she's already gone. See the difference?

Will there be times when you'll want to use passive or inactive verbs? Yes, of course. I'm not telling you not to. But if you do a search and you find that you have an excessive amount of 'was going's' or 'started to's' in your manuscript, you may want to look at your verb choices and make some changes. Use inactive and passive verbs sparingly and purposefully.

Using Description to Achieve Deep Point of View

Description is as much about the feeling, person or object being described as it is about the character doing the actual describing. Deep POV is seeing and experiencing the world through a character's eyes. Deep point of view draws the reader into the story. It inserts them into the action, putting the reader into the head and heart of your characters. Let's have a look at how you can achieve deep point of view through description.

Male vs. Female POV

Generally...men tend to use shorter, to the point sentences. Women tend to use longer, more descriptive sentences. A man might say 'The house is blue.' A woman might say 'The house is light blue with dark blue trim, gingerbread around the porch and a red roof.' Unless the man was an architect or remodeled houses for a living or as a hobby. In that case he might go into more detail about the house because of his profession.

This is especially important in describing emotions. Men and women can react to similar situations in very different ways. A male character might *act* angry without actually acknowledging the fact that he's mad. Your description of his behavior will tip off the reader to what is really happening with him. Similarly a juvenile character might be a know-it-all to disguise the fact that he's deeply insecure. Or a female character might act overly happy to fool others into believing that her life is as perfect as it appears.

The way the author describes a character's actions, reactions, tone, and timbre will give the reader clues as to how a character is *really* feeling. Don't be clichéd when it comes to gender or age. Incongruous behaviors and feelings can add depth to your characters and story line.

Point of View Shifts: Less Is More

The longer you keep the reader in the head of one character, the deeper the connection to that character grows. This is especially important in description, as description gives the reader insight not only into what a person/place/thing looks like, but how the character doing the describing thinks, feels, and perceives that person/place/thing. Use description to show the reader *who* your character is and how they're feeling. Immerse your reader in your character's experiences and emotions before introducing them to a different character.

There is no set page or paragraph minimum or maximum for POV shifts, but if you head hop more than once or twice in a scene you may confuse your reader. POV shifts should be deliberate and done for a specific reason.

I could write a whole book on point of view and how, when, and why an author would want to switch POV and what effect that would have on the scene and the reader. For now, I just want you to be aware of this tool and how description can play a part.

Using the Five Senses in Description

Using the five senses—scent, sight, sound, touch, taste—in description grounds the reader in the scene. Sensory description enriches the reader experience, especially when tied to things the reader would be familiar with—the smell of fresh baked cookies, the sound of a heart beat, the sight of a beautiful sunset, the touch of a mother's hand, the tart taste of an apple.

As E.L. Doctorow said, "Good writing is supposed to evoke sensation in the reader—not the fact that it is raining, but the feeling of being rained upon."

Sight

Most novels (with the exception of children's books) lack photos or drawings to give the reader a visual. It's up to you, the writer, to draw those pictures with your words. Creating vivid imagery is very important in description. In fact, it's the one element people think of most when they think of description. But humans don't experience the world by sight alone. We have four other senses that feed us information and help us navigate through our day to day lives. Vision is just one way we assimilate information about all manner of things from the weather, a location, a building, an object or a person.

A visual description alone is not enough to draw the reader into your scene. What if it's too dark for your character to see anything? What if your character is blind? How would that character describe his world? Challenge yourself to not rely solely on visuals in your description.

Scent

Smell is the most nostalgic of the senses and can help your reader identify with your character in unexpected ways. With scent you can call up past experiences and memories for your character and your reader—the smell of a father's aftershave, the scent of freshly mowed grass, the aroma of grandma's apple pie—you get the idea. It's all very sentimental and can be a moment of shared experience for your reader.

Sound

Unless your character is experiencing sound deprivation or is deaf, there will be noise in their world. In fact, the absence of sound in a setting can give your character and your reader a sense that something is very wrong—a jungle that goes suddenly quiet or the secession of chatter when a character enters a room. Using sound in description gives the reader more information about the world you've created—traffic noise in a city or the screech of seagulls at the beach.

Comparing one sound to another in description can be very effective—the wail of an ambulance was like a child's scream in the dead of night. It creates an immediate, identifiable sound for your reader.

Touch

There are two different kinds of touches in description—the way something *feels* and the sensation of *being touched*. Touch can be either pleasurable or painful or in some cases—a combination of both. The way something feels to your character and the comparisons they might make using past experiences can reveal things about your characters to the reader. A hot, sweaty handshake can say something about a character's emotions that a cool, dry hand can't. Using touch to draw comparisons between things can be quite interesting—a cold headstone on a sweltering summer day, for example.

How a character reacts to being touched physically is a great way to tap into emotions that can have roots in a character's backstory. Does your character like being touched or are they uncomfortable with it? Is your character the touchy-feely type or do they use touch sparingly with meaning? Touch is a very important sense in sex scenes. It can elevate the scene from playful to deeply sensual, depending on the type of touch.

Taste

Taste is most often used when a character is eating and drinking or kissing and making love—occasions when they'll be using their mouths and tongues. There are other, more unexpected times when you can use the sense of taste in description—the coppery, metallic taste of blood, a salty ocean breeze, the mouthwatering expectation of your mother's meatloaf. Look for unexpected ways to use taste in place of one of the other senses in your descriptions.

The Sixth Sense

The unscientific sixth sense can be used to foreshadow events or alert a character to something wrong that could protect them from danger. Don't confuse this sense with an omniscient point of view. Make sure your character is experiencing this sense and you're not intruding as an author.

Little did Mary know, but a bad guy was hiding around the corner.

That's not using the sixth sense. That's author intrusion.

The fine hairs on Mary's neck stood on end and she had the uncomfortable sensation of being watched.

That's using the sixth sense. We get a strong feeling just as Mary does that something isn't right. Could be a bad guy hiding around the corner or it could be a raccoon watching her. As a reader we don't know and that's okay. What happens next will fill in the blanks for the reader.

Using More Than One Sense in Description

Using more than one sense in a description can

have a powerful effect and deepen the reader's experience. Try to employ at least two—if not or more—of the five senses in your scenes. This isn't a license to bust out all five senses in one scene. You'll overwhelm your reader.

Here are some examples of using more than one sense in a description and the powerful emotions you can conjure in a scene.

From **How to Bake a Perfect Life** by Barbara O'Neal:

A collection of blue bottles, large and small, was lined up on the windowsill. Sandwiched between them were small clay pots filled with herbs. When the sun was on them, like now, they made the air smell like root beer and Thanksgiving morning.

In this scene, Ms. O'Neal not only gives the reader a visual, she's creates an evocative scent to ground the reader. We all know what Thanksgiving and root beer smell like, but put together we really begin to picture the windowsill and the room, coloring in the scene with our own emotions and scent memories.

From **Vindicate** by Beth Yarnall:
When he's close like this I forget why

things could never work out between us. His scent wraps around me in the small space. I breathe him in and it's like he's a part of me. The stroke of his thumb across my cheek echoes in other parts of my body and I feel myself leaning into him like a flower seeks the sun. I don't want any of this and yet it's all *I want.*

Here we have scent combined with touch, which is often used in love scenes. We're naturally drawn to a mate whose DNA is very different than ours and one of the ways we do that is through smelling the pheromones they give off. It's an inborn instinct to ensure our offspring are the strongest and healthiest they can be.

According to Desmond Morris's *Intimate Behaviour: A Zoologist's Classic Study of Human Intimacy*, there are twelve levels of intimacy that escalate from one (eye to body glance) to twelve (intercourse). A hand to face touch is a level eight on the intimacy scale and is considered more intimate than a kiss, which clocks in at level seven. So in this scene we've got a pretty powerful touch combined with a very strong reaction to scent. A one two punch.

Setting the Scene

Description can be used to set a scene and ground the reader in the world they're entering. You'll often see this at the beginning of a book and/or at the beginning of a scene. When a character enters a new world the reader wants to be able to imagine it. In genres such as SciFi, Fantasy, Dystopian or Paranormal, setting the scene for the reader is very important. You're building the world in which your characters and your readers will live. Don't be ordinary. Don't be clichéd. Don't use the first descriptive words that come to mind.

Example from **Scandal of the Black Rose** by Debra Mullins:

Sunlight shone in multicolored hues through the stained-glass windows of the church. The glow warmed the golden brown wood of the pews lining either side of the aisle before her, and dust motes danced like faeries in the sweep of light.

You can see the church, can't you? Notice the lack of exacting detail. Ms. Mullins didn't describe the number of pews in each row or mark off how large the church is because that's not what's important. What's important about this description is the image it draws and the way it makes the reader feel. You can picture it. Maybe it's like a church you went to as a child. Even though there is no scent description the reader can imagine how the church might smell and if it's warm or cool inside.

This description sets the mood of the scene. Nothing bad could happen in a church like this...or could it?

From **Angelfall** by Susan Ee:

Ironically, since the attacks, the sunsets have been glorious. Outside our condo window, the sky flames like a bruised mango in vivid orange, red, and purple. The clouds ignite with sunset colors, and I'm almost scared those of us caught below will catch on fire too.

These are the opening lines of the book. They instantly grab your attention. She doesn't say it outright, but we get the sense that this is another world than the one we live in. Look at her word choices—like a *bruised* mango, the sky *flames*, the clouds *ignite*, those of us *caught* below will *catch fire*. What does the word choice show the reader about the world he's about to enter? This description of a sunset is fresh and unexpected yet easily imagined. Can't you see the vivid colors? Can't you feel the ominousness of the ironic change *since the attacks*?

Setting the scene with an attention grabbing, compelling description can do a lot for your story. This is your opportunity to draw your world for your reader. Fully imagine the room your character is about to walk into. What does it look like? What does it feel like? How does your character feel in that space? Bad things can happen in good places and vice versa. Give your reader the whole picture. Make it interesting. Draw your reader in. Then let the action happen.

Word Choice Matters

Word choice is especially important in description. Showing vs. telling, not using filtering words that separate the reader from your characters, and using descriptive verbs are ways you can draw the reader deeper into your characters' experiences.

The Dreaded Adverb

So avoid using the word 'very' because it's lazy. A man is not very tired, he is exhausted. Don't use very sad, use morose. Language was invented for one reason, boys—to woo women—and, in that endeavor laziness will not do. ~ Dead Poet's Society

Mark Twain said, "Substitute *damn* every time you're inclined to write *very*; your editor will delete it and the writing will be just as it should be."

The overuse of very and –ly words is a sign of an amateur or lazy writer. Should you *never* use adverbs? No. Of course not. Sometimes it's more expedient to write *she knocked softly*. Everything you write doesn't have to be flowery and beautiful. Remember, description is used to draw your reader's attention to something that is important to the story. If there was no significance to *how* she knocked, such as creating tension or suspense in the scene, then you could just as easily write *she knocked on the door*. It's a longer transitional action, but it basically achieves the same thing.

When you use adverbs, do so sparingly and with purpose and only if you can't find a way to rewrite the sentence using stronger, more descriptive verbs and adjectives.

He lazily walked down the corridor. vs. He ambled down the corridor.

She entered the room quietly. vs. She crept into the room.

He's very ugly. vs. He's hideous.

Do a search of your manuscript. Look for adverbs and rewrite wherever you can. Here's a list of commonly over and misused adverbs:

- accusingly
- adamantly
- angrily
- argumentatively
- automatically
- badly
- beautifully
- boldly

- breathlessly
- carefully
- certainly
- correctly
- dangerously
- effortlessly
- generally
- generously
- gladly
- gracefully
- greatly
- happily
- heartily
- highly
- horrifyingly
- hungrily
- ironically
- literally
- loudly
- lovely
- lowly
- massively
- motionlessly
- mournfully
- necessarily
- normally
- only
- painstakingly
- partially

- perfectly
- practically
- pragmatically
- promptly
- proudly
- quickly
- quietly
- really
- roughly
- sadly
- separately
- sharply
- shortly
- slowly
- smoothly
- softly
- spitefully
- suddenly
- thankfully
- very
- wrongly

Watch for –ly words that state the obvious—she yelled loudly. If she's yelling, she's being loud. He stumbled awkwardly—is there any other way to stumble? He's bald headed—he's bald *and* he has a head, redundant. Her past history—isn't everyone's past history?

Let's talk about the word *literally*. I've

found that most things in life aren't as literal as the overuse and misuse of the word literally. It's crept into our verbal lexicon, but it rarely has a place in a fiction novel. Both readers and editors often list the word literally as a pet peeve. Delete it and then read your sentence out loud. I'd bet money that the sentence doesn't suffer the loss.

Now go forth and slay those –ly dragons wherever you can.

Keeping It Fresh

Similes and metaphors are powerful tools in description, but be careful. They can quickly morph into clichés. You have access to a vast and varied language—the English language. Use it all. Use it in unexpected and unusual ways. Think outside of the box (cliché!). Just because a word is normally used in a particular way doesn't mean you have to use it that way. Open your mind to new ways of saying the same old thing.

Similes and Metaphors

The use of similes and metaphors can really up the wow factor of your descriptions and are used to create colorful imagery. Both similes and metaphors compare one thing to another with similes using the words *like* or *as* to make those associations whereas metaphors do not.

Similes

From **Dyed and Gone** by Beth Yarnall:

Juan Carlos made a sound like *a balloon losing air.*

An easily imagined sound. Everyone... Okay, almost everyone, knows what that high-pitched noise sounds like. There's no other explanation needed.

From **Lush** by Beth Yarnall:

She resisted at first and then it was as if her body recalled his as well, and she came at him like *a bull out of a chute, going from zero to all over him in thirty seconds or less.*

Another comparison that nearly every reader can imagine. A little side note: This book is set in Dallas. The use of *like a bull out of a chute* was used purposefully as it has meaning for the characters and is appropriate for where they live. If the book were set in Hawaii this simile might not make as much sense.

Metaphors

From **Vindicate** by Beth Yarnall:

"God, Cora." His voice is a sigh that arrows straight through me, fanning out into tiny prickles of pleasure and pain.

The sigh doesn't literally pierce her body, but we get a very clear picture of the effect the tone of his voice has on her emotionally, which manifests physically. A double whammy. Be original (am I starting to sound like a broken record?) in your comparisons. Make the reader feel what your character is feeling as they're feeling it.

From **Vindicate** by Beth Yarnall:

Her words are a sucker punch to the gut.

Again, this is not a literal punch to the stomach. It's a figurative one. Her words shock and hurt him. He didn't see them coming. We get all of that from this metaphor.

Here's a test. Is this next example a simile or a metaphor?

From **Atone** by Beth Yarnall:

All lace and silk, she's sweet looking in her soft colors like she just walked out of a Sunday church service.

If you guessed simile you're correct.

Now your turn. Try your hand at writing a simile and a metaphor using your characters. You can compare an emotion, a facial expression, appearance or anything else you'd like.

Have fun with similes and metaphors, but again, don't over do it and watch out for clichés. Your character might *drink like a fish*, but I bet you can find another way to describe that without resorting to the usual. Speaking of clichés...

Clichés

Avoid overused words and phrases when describing. These especially crop up when using similes and metaphors. Clichés are a sign of writer newness or laziness. Be creative. Don't use the first word or phrase that comes to mind because it's probably a cliché. Dig deep for fresh description and don't be afraid to use words in new ways.

Common clichés -- nails on a chalkboard, butterflies in the stomach, sleeping like the dead, screaming like a Banshee, heavy as lead, wrack your brain, calm before the storm, and so on. They're called clichés because we've all heard them a thousand and one times. Here are some descriptions that are *not* clichéd.

From **Dark Wild Night** by Christina Lauren:

Even having never kissed him—beyond the quick, soft kiss at our sham-of-a-wedding—I know I would be worse off if I had him for a week and then lost him. My heart would be warped afterward, like a wool sweater loaned to a body too big and growing misshapen until it doesn't fit quite right anymore.

A very fresh simile. I love this description. There's nothing ordinary about it. She really likes him and nothing short of having him will do. This writing duo could've just stated that the heroine was falling for the hero, but they chose to show this to the reader in a unique and unexpected way.

From **The Opportunist** by Tarryn Fisher:

Her jowls flap around like pillowcases

and I snicker.

This simile makes me laugh just like the character does. We can't take the jowly character seriously and it's a very different way of saying that this character talks too much.

From **Dirty Red** by Tarryn Fisher:

My mother was walking toward us, each of her birdlike steps tugging a fresh strand of dread to the forefront of my mind.

Not clichéd *at all*. We get a very clear picture of how this character's mother makes her feel as well as a sense of the type of person the mother is.

From **Dark Wild Night** by Christina Lauren:

My mind is a blender, coherent thoughts are chopped and killed.

A brilliant metaphor that is anything *but* clichéd. There are some powerful emotions at play here in this character's head.

If you're having trouble describing something, find a picture of it. Study it. Then find a new way of showing your reader what it looks like. *She had blue eyes* isn't going to cut it. Make your reader *see* the intensity of her blue eyes and the power of her stare and what it does to your hero. If you're having trouble describing a sound, go online and find a snippet of it. You can find all kinds of sounds from a helicopter to the screech of an owl. Listen to the sound, then find a fresh, new way to describe it. Compound descriptions—a description that conjures an image in the reader's mind and lets him or her know how the character is feeling—are *never* clichéd.

Getting Emotional

One of the most common mistakes new writers make is that they *tell* the reader what the character is feeling instead of *showing* them—he was angry, she was sad, they were afraid. To have your readers fully immersed in your characters and their story, they have to feel what your character feels *while* they're feeling it. Their hearts have to pound as fear grips your character. Their eyes have to well with tears as your character despairs.

Visceral or Physical Reactions

Emotions often evoke physical or visceral reactions such as a pounding heart, sweaty hands or a sick stomach (clichés!). Using physical reactions to display emotion in your description shows the reader what your character is feeling without you having to point out the emotion.

From **Dark Wild Night** by Christina

Lauren:

The memory trips a fluttery, anxious beat in my chest.

This description is the non-clichéd version of a pounding heart.

From **Hot Head** by Damon Suede:

It was like sand in his sheets, the nagging fear that he'd overlook a detail and his adopted family would die, leaving him trapped in the basement of his father's empty house.

Everyone knows what sand in the sheets feels like or they can at least imagine how irritating it is. Using a familiar sensation grounds the reader. Comparing it to fear is a terrific combination. This description goes one step further in that it shows the reader that the fear is probably greater than the character is admitting. The author made subtle use of who the character is—a man—in this description. *His family would die, leaving him trapped*--that's more than a *nagging fear* or the discomfort of *sand in your sheets*. Men will often downplay their emotions and are not as likely to fully admit certain emotions such as fear or doubt even to themselves.

From **Dark Wild** Night by Christina Lauren:

The words incinerate my lungs and I stop breathing again. There isn't a word for what I'm feeling. It is the direct, razor edge of ecstasy and terror.

Nice metaphor here—*the words incinerate my lungs*. The character tries to sort out what she's feeling, but it's so intense that she can't decide if it's ecstasy or terror. A very powerful description of emotion.

Telling vs. Showing...Again

Another way writers show their newness is in writing emotion. There are ways you can show your reader what your character is feeling without having to resort to blurting it out and moving on.

Here is a short, four sentence scene that tells the reader what is happening. At the same time it doesn't give *any* emotional context. The reader isn't going to care what happens to the character in the scene nor should they.

She heard his footsteps on the stairs.

What to do? She threw the latch on the door and backed away from it. She was going to be in for it this time.

There's lots of telling in that passage, isn't there? Not to mention we have no real clue about how she's really feeling, who she is, who's coming up the stairs, or who these people are to each other.

Now we're going to take the same number of sentences (four) and rewrite the passage so that it *shows* what the character is feeling when she hears those footsteps on the stairs.

Example #1 of showing:

The lightness of his boots on the stairs sent the butterflies in her stomach into overdrive. Wondering what to do, she looked for a way to get him back for all the tricks he'd played on her. Wanting to extend the game, she could hardly get her fingers to work the latch, but finally managed it, suppressing a bubble of laughter as she backed away from the door. She was going to be in for it this time.

There's a ton of clues as to what is happening in this scene, isn't there? It's light and playful. These people are having fun. Take a look at the word choices—lightness, butterflies, wonder(ing), tricks, played, game, bubble, laughter. Aren't you wondering how he's going to pay her back? You're invested in the scene because you feel what the character is feeling.

Now let's change it up. Here's the same scene rewritten with a totally different tone.

Example #2 of showing:

The thud of his boots on the stairs pounded in her ears. Her heart fluttered like a captured bird in her chest as she frantically wondered what to do. With numbed fingers she threw the latch on the door and backed away from it, prickles of dread racing up her spine. She was going to be in for it this time.

Ooooo, a totally different scene, isn't it? There's suspense, tension, and fear in this scene. Let's take a look at the word choices— thud, pounded, captured, frantically, numbed, prickles, dread. This is a totally different relationship between these characters than in the first example. Are you worried for her? Are you concerned about what he's going to do to her when he catches her? If I did my job right, you should be.

There's lots of showing in both examples.

It's amazing how changing the description completely changes the tone of the scene. The same actions are happening in both scenes, but they are *very* different because of the description. Both descriptions work hard to instill certain emotions in the reader, drawing them deeper into the scene, making them care about what happens next to the character.

From **A Night to Surrender** by Tessa Dare:

The sultry rasp in his voice had persuasive force. It moved her center of balance, rocking her from her toes to her heels. She took a step in reverse, and her back met the wall of ancient stone. A cool ridge calmed the place between her shoulder blades.

What do you think she's feeling in this passage? She's aroused and maybe a little nervous, but she's not afraid. The timbre of his voice physically moved her, unbalancing her. This is a very subtle description with lots of showing and subtext.

From **The Opportunist** by Tarryn Fisher:

My heart is beating so fast, I can feel it

pounding in my kneecaps.

This description makes me smile. Definitely not clichéd.

From **How to Misbehave** by Ruthie Knox:

In the dark, silence had a completely different quality. She felt exposed, her heart beating over a loudspeaker, her words echoing in the space between them.

A strong visceral reaction to something that many people are afraid of—the dark. The reader can easily identify with what the character is feeling in this description.

From **Dark Wild Night** by Christina Lauren:

I feel the cold prick of panic spread across my neck, nausea bubbles in my belly. The two conversations—with Oliver, with Austin—are oil and vinegar, splashing around in my thoughts.

A great metaphoric comparison and fresh use of words, comparing oil and vinegar to thoughts that refuse to coexist in the same headspace. When I talk about using ordinary words in unusual ways this is exactly what I mean.

Readers won't put a book down or throw it across the room because it makes them *feel* too much. Even when the emotions get intense and your reader has to take a break, they will come back to your book. I'm reminded of that TV episode of *Friends* where Joey had to put the Stephen King book in the freezer because it scared him too much. He pulled it out and continued reading it though. Emotion hooks readers and makes them want to stay in your world as long as possible.

Physical Description

Authors often forget that it's not them doing the describing—it's their character. Nowhere else does an author get it wrong the most than when they're writing physical description. Physical description shouldn't read like a laundry list of traits—long red hair...check. Violet eyes...check (and clichéd). Strong chiseled jaw...check. Lock of raven hair over one eye...check. *yawns* *Boring*.

Be stealthy with physical description. Don't draw the reader's attention to it. Tie physical description into how the describing character thinks or feels about the person they're describing. This is your opportunity to show your reader *more*.

Perception and Judgment

Physical description is about perception and judgment. How a character perceives and judges his world and the people in it says a lot about him. This is when the description goes beyond what is being described. Perception is your character making assumptions about what he sees, hears, smells, touches, and tastes based on his experiences. Judgment is your character forming an opinion based on those perceptions. Everybody has an opinion, right? What is your character's opinion? Why is it important to the story? Is their first impression correct or incorrect? There's lots of room to play with perception and judgment when it comes to physical description. After all, our society is based on looks.

From **How to Bake a Perfect Life** by Barbara O'Neal:

She still didn't have a bra on, and everything about her seemed like a warning—her eccentricities, her husbandlessness, her offbeat everything.

Lots of perception going on here—*seemed like a warning*. And a fair bit of judgment—*her eccentricities, her husbandlessness, her offbeat everything*. Husbandlessness isn't a real word. Husbandless is. Kudos to the author for being creative and pioneering in her work and for using words in unexpected ways. Shakespeare made up many of the words we use everyday.

Why can't *we* be just as inventive?

From **Tempting a Proper Lady** by Debra Mullins:

Though he wore sophisticated evening black, something about him read untamed. *Was it his ink black hair, slightly too long for fashion? The sun-browned skin of his face and hands? His powerful build, made more impressive by the elegant cut of his clothing? Or maybe it was the go-to-the-devil look in his dark eyes?*

Ah, inconsistencies. He's conforming to societal parameters and yet he doesn't fit in. We get some physical description with *ink black hair, sun-browned skin,* and *dark eyes,* but it's cleverly woven in with other more important description. We have an idea of not only what he looks like physically, but the type of person he might be and a touch of how he makes the heroine feel—she's intrigued (and so is the reader).

From **Rush** by Beth Yarnall:

He could tell the woman had been beautiful in her youth, but her face had been gouged deep by the hard edges of life. She'd made a valiant effort to recapture her looks with makeup, but had overdone it, reminding Lucas of a paint-by-numbers portrait. Red lipstick bled into the creases around her mouth and when she kissed Mi on the cheek she left a stain, like a lonely lip print on an empty shot glass.

A heavy dose of perception and judgment here with very little physical description other than the overdone makeup. But that's not what's important here. How does the hero feel about this woman who he's meeting for the first time? Would you be surprised to know that she's the heroine's mother? He doesn't have a high opinion of her, does he? Could his harsh perception and judgment affect his relationship with the heroine?

Characters Describing Other Characters

I said it before, I'll say it again... less is more. You don't need to remind your reader about your hero's eye color or your heroine's hair color every other scene. What's most important about character description is how the other characters see each other and how they see themselves. And I'm not necessarily talking about physical traits.

The hero describing the heroine at the beginning of the story...

From **A Deep and Dark December** by Beth Yarnall:

Still, she was beautiful. There was a fragility to her that belied her fiery personality. She looked made of china, the kind his Grandma Byrne only put out on special occasions because it was fine and old, having passed through several generations. And like the danger of handling his grandma's china, he had to suppress the urge to touch her, run the tips of his fingers along her jaw, her collarbone. Half the time he wasn't sure she was real. Something as delicate as she belonged to the faery stories Grandma Byrne had told him as a boy.

This description does more than show the reader what the heroine looks like; it also shows how the hero feels about her. He sees her as delicate and fragile, right? This description is important because by the end of the story the hero will come to depend a great deal on the heroine's strength.

Did you notice that nowhere in that description is the color of the heroine's eyes or hair? Why is that?

1) that's not what was important at this point in the story (chapter two)

2) men don't often go into that kind of detail.

I found out a few years ago that my husband had no idea what color my eyes are... and we'd been together for more than 20 years. If he described me to someone he likely wouldn't describe detailed things about me like my eye color. Is this always the rule with men? No. But it's an interesting thing to consider when writing description. What kinds of things would your character notice or not notice?

From **Dyed and Gone** by Beth Yarnall:

Pale as the moon and framed by hair darker than night, Trinity's face was eerily perfect, freakish in its symmetry as if it had been made by a machine. I supposed some would have called her beautiful with features exactly the size and shape as they should be. But there was something wrong, something altogether ugly and unstable about the way they came together.

Again, there's not a lot of detail, is there? What does the heroine think of the woman she's describing? How does the woman make the heroine *feel*? This description is all about the sensations our heroine has upon meeting this woman. The reader is given clues based on the words I chose to use—*eerily, freakish, wrong, ugly and unstable.* Could I have just come out and told the reader that the woman is mentally ill? Sure. But that's boring. I'd rather show the reader and make them feel the heroine's unease.

From **Dark Wild Night** by Christina Lauren:

When I look at him—wide grin, fingers flying in a ridiculous air guitar, lip curled like a rocker—I realize his glasses break up his looks, cool them down, add ice to the glass. Without them, he's all bone structure and color: brilliant blue eyes, warm lips, coffee-brown stubble.

She's seeing him in a different way. How your character describes the other characters in your book should change and evolve as the story moves along, as they get to know each other. An *other* realization if you will, a deepening of the connection they're forming. This description does a good job of showing that progression.

From **A Deep and Dark December** by Beth Yarnall:
Mabel hesitated, causing Erin to look up.

Her expression said everything. Mabel had never been good at hedging. Donald had made a comment once about Mabel's inability to keep her emotions from showing on her face. Something about the honesty of it and how he always knew where he stood with her. Erin thought the woman had never bothered to perfect her poker face so that people would ask her what was wrong and she could tell them the latest gossip with complete impunity. After all, they'd asked.

What does Erin *really* think of Mabel? She's cunning, a gossiper, a woman with an agenda, right? And Erin isn't at all fooled by her like her father, Donald, is. Would it surprise you to know that Mabel is her father's girlfriend? Knowing that changes the tone of the description, doesn't it?

When a Character Describes Him or Herself

In first person a character description is a lot trickier than in third person. The most clichéd way for an author to describe a character in first person is by having their protagonist look a mirror or at a photo of themself while thinking about how brown their hair is and how blue are their eyes. Real people never do that.

Think for a moment about how you would

describe yourself. You'd probably be pretty critical, right? We are hardest on ourselves, after all. You'd probably focus on your flaws and unfavorably compare yourself to others, right? It's natural. Unfortunately it's what we do. So if you have a character go on and on about how beautiful she is or how ruggedly built he is, then your description and character will not ring true with your reader. Your reader may not even *like* your character. After all, who likes people who go on and on about how great they are?

A little self-deprecation goes a long way in first person.

From **Wake Up Maggie** by Beth Yarnall:

We lay in the aftermath, sheets and clothes strewn all around. A fine sheen of sweat coated his body, highlighting the rises and lowlighting the valleys. He looked like he'd been sculpted from fine stone. Whereas I looked like I'd been molded out of Playdoh by an art-challenged toddler. My hair, unruly on most days, now lay in tangled ropes around us, but I hardly cared about any of that with the zing of multiple orgasms still jolting my system.

Notice again the lack of detail. But what we get is a clear picture of how Maggie sees herself slipped in with a little physical description of the hero and how she's feeling about what just happened. She's making an unfair yet normal comparison between her and him. In first person there won't be a whole lot of detailed physical description unless it's another character remarking on your protagonist's looks. Be okay with that if you write first person.

Now hold up your right hand and solemnly swear that you will no longer write physical description as a boring laundry list of traits. Let your cover carry some of the physical description duty. Be inventive. Don't feel like you have to give a detailed physical description of all of your characters. Leave something to your reader's imagination. Give them room to imagine themselves as your hero or heroine.

Deconstructing Looks, Gestures, and Expressions

Expressions, looks, and gestures are opportunities to show your reader who your characters are or how they're perceived. They're often the most underused tools in a writer's toolbox. Don't be bland by using the old standbys—he grinned, she looked at him, she gestured wildly, he frowned. Boring. *Show* your reader more.

When a Smile Is More Than a Smile

There are as many different kinds of smiles as there are emotions. Does a smile always mean that a character is happy? Or could it reveal something else about the character's personality or thoughts? Smiles and grins are both overused and underused, meaning it's one of the most commonly used dialog tags by authors, and yet a lot of authors waste the opportunity to let the smile show their reader *more* about their character and the scene.

From **A Deep and Dark December** by Beth Yarnall:

"You're not dressed," Keith said when Erin opened the door to him at their appointed date time. "Not that you don't look great." He gave her his charming smile, the one he reserved for difficult customers at the store.

Is he happy with her? What is he really thinking? We're not in his point of view, but from the protagonist's description of his smile we know that he's not happy about having to wait for her. Also what does this passage tell us about him? Hint: He's the manager of a store. This goes all the way back to chapter one where we talked about who a character was and who they are now. This smile is working hard for me in the story.

From **A Deep and Dark December** by Beth Yarnall:

Graham rolled his head her direction, one corner of his mouth kicked up and he had a naughty gleam in his eye that was probably the undoing of a lot of ladies' intentions.

Another kind of smile, right? A naughty

smile that will possibly be the undoing of her intentions. She can't resist him when he smiles like that.

From **Ruin** by Rachel Van Dyken:

His eyes were a pale blue, his hair a golden blond that was a little too long and curled by his ears. And his smile. Well, his smile would probably haunt me for the rest of my life. It was easy, and his dimples only made it worse. And then there was his smell. A mixture of some cinnamon and something else I couldn't really put my finger on. It irritated me how easy it seemed for him to smile, as if nothing was wrong in the world when everything felt like it inside. He wanted to shake my hand and know my name and I wanted to get the hell out of there and sit in my room, preferably rocking back and forth in a corner until my anti-depressants decided to kick into high gear.

This description is all about *her* not him. The ease with which he smiles unnerves her. *He* unnerves her. We get that message loud and clear.

Smiles are not throwaways. In fact, nothing in your novel should be throwaway (except for the word *said*, which is basically invisible to the reader). Why is your character smiling? What does that smile tell us about his thoughts and mood? What does it tell the *other* characters about his thoughts and mood? I challenge you to be judicious with smiles and to make them count for more in your story.

Look, Gaze, Stare, Glance, and Generally Give the Eye To

The kind of look a character gives another character can reveal a lot about them—what they're thinking and how they're feeling as well as the kind of person they are. This is another dialog tag a lot of authors throw away when they shouldn't. It's amateur. *He looked at her*— not good enough. Of course he's looking at her if they're in the same room, having a conversation. Where else would he look? At the floor, the wall, the ceiling? If a character looks away make it be for a reason. If he looks back make that also happen for a reason. What was said or done to make him look away? What drew his attention back?

Use looks to ratchet up tension in scenes and to disclose something about your character to your reader.

From **Heaven, Texas** by Susan

Elizabeth Phillips:

Bobby Tom paused at the door and gave his agent that level, blue-eyed gaze defensive players all over the league had learned to dread.

Is this a guy to be messed with? No. He's the kind of guy who expects to get his way and usually does. This look says much more about him than if the author had written *Bobby Tom paused at the door and looked at his agent.* Snore!

From **Rush** by Beth Yarnall:

"Just no." She looked out to where her mother stood by a fire truck, smoothing the blanket over her cheek. "This is not your problem."

Then a little later in the conversation...

Her gazed whipped to his, her eyes red rimmed and sharp with anger. "Let it go."

Ah-ha! Something that was said or done made her look away, then something was said to make her look back with this strong reaction. Do you see what I mean about people looking away and then back at each other? There was thought and intent behind the shifting glances. They did more than serve as dialog tags to denote who is speaking. The heroine is hiding something from the hero. She's trying to avoid this conversation. She doesn't want his help.

Tying Emotions Into Gestures

Characters, like real people, will often have a gesture or habit they consciously or unconsciously repeat. Nail biting, jiggling change, rocking back on their heels, etc. Use gestures to show what your character is feeling.

From **Vindicate** by Beth Yarnall:

Beau looks away, picking at the side of his thumb with his index finger. Even as a kid he always did this whenever he was agitated or annoyed. "I don't need it."

This gesture tells us something about what Beau is feeling and about his relationship with the heroine. They're siblings, but even if you didn't know that, you would know they've known each other since they were kids.

From **Scandal of the Black Rose** by

Debra Mullins:

Last night's near disaster haunted her still, and she found herself more than once stroking the familiar cameo of her newly repaired locket between her fingers in an old gesture of anxiety.

We now know that stroking her cameo calms her so that when she does it later in the book, we know she's feeling anxious or uncertain.

Be certain the gesture your character is using fits the scene. Study what different body language means. I once read a really emotional scene a friend wrote. The hero was coming clean, finally revealing himself to the heroine. In a dialog tag she had the hero stand across the room with his hands in his pockets. That's an outward sign of someone with something to hide. So in this big reveal scene his body language contradicted what he was saying. Which is a great way to show that the character is either lying or hiding something. But if that's not what was intended, then you might confuse your reader.

Gestures are important. Like gazes and smiles, they're not throwaway descriptions in dialog tags. They can back up what your character is saying or completely negate it. Be sure the gestures you give your characters are conveying what you intended for the scene.

Clues, Guesstimations, and Assumptions

We don't know what everyone else around us is thinking, but we can guess by their expressions, actions, tone of voice, and word choice. The same goes for your characters. When you're in your character's POV you're looking at the world through *their* eyes. What clues do they pick up from the other characters in the book? How do they process those clues? What conclusions do they draw from the clues? Use description to give your characters those clues.

Visual Clues

From **A Night to Surrender** by Tessa Dare:

Their gazes locked and held. Something defensive flared in those bold green eyes, and she wondered at the thoughts crossing his mind. Not thoughts of kissing her, she'd wager.

I'd wager not too! He reacted to

something she said or did and now she's wondering what he's thinking. You can use that unknown to your advantage. Your character can guess correctly or guess incorrectly or wait until they get more from the other character before deciding. Have fun with it.

From **Reclaim** by Beth Yarnall:

"Hey." She gives me a cursory once-over and I can't tell a damn thing from her expression. "I passed a Starbucks a block or so back. That okay?"

Ever have that happen to you? Somebody looks you up and down and you have no idea what he or she thinks of you. Makes you nervous, doesn't it? Especially in a new relationship. You want them to like you, but you're just not sure. Use that, play with it.

Tone of Voice and Inflection

How a character says something goes beyond the words that are spoken. Tone is everything. Use description to give readers and your characters insight as to what is really being said. Sometimes inflection can negate what is being said and sometimes it can support it, depending on what you're trying to achieve in the scene.

From **Dirty Red** by Tarryn Fisher:

"Leah." His voice touched my name in a way that made me close my eyes. Everything that rolled off his tongue sounded beautiful but especially my name.

That one word—her name—has a powerful effect on her just because of the way he says it. Also the phrase *his voice touched my name* is an inventive way of saying *he said my name*. This is a great example of using words in new and unexpected ways. His voice can't touch, but using the word *touch* makes the saying of her name feel much more intimate.

From **Atone** by Beth Yarnall:

"Vera." He says my name softly, with care, as though it's a fragile thing.

A very different tone of voice here, but the way he says her name makes her feel cherished and special, doesn't it?

From **How to Misbehave** by Ruthie

Knox:

His voice didn't sound right. It sounded as if it was pushing back against the weight of something, but that didn't make any sense.

She only has his voice in the dark to tell her he's anxious and scared. Something in his voice tips her off. I also love the phrasing here *sounded as if it was pushing back against the weight of something.* A very unusual and fresh way of showing the reader his fear without saying *he sounded scared.*

From **Atone** by Beth Yarnall:

"No one's ever said that to me and actually meant it." There's shame in her tone, as if it's her *fault no one's ever loved her before.*

If I've done my job, your heart should be breaking a little bit for both of them. Does it make you wonder about her and what happened to her to make her feel this way?

Do your characters' actions always match their words? Visual clues can also be conflicting or misread, leading to some very interesting complications for your characters. Conflicting actions and words can reveal a lot about a character. It's like the old saying—actions speak louder than words. Your characters can reveal their true feelings or thoughts in this way.

From **A Deep and Dark December** by Beth Yarnall:

"Oh, I get it." He relaxed back, laughing a little, his cheeks pinkening. "We should have talked about this sooner. It's nothing to be embarrassed about."

He's telling her not to be embarrassed as he flushes in embarrassment. Who's he trying to convince, him or her?

From **A Night to Surrender** by Tessa Dare:

"Oh, no reason." Payne rubbed his mouth with one hand, as if massaging away a laugh. "Please, do go on."

He's laughing internally at what's being said and trying to conceal it. His words *no reason* contradict the rubbing away of his smile. There's a reason and he's hiding his amusement. Don't you wonder why?

Your characters can draw some fun,

confusing, nerve-wracking conclusions based on the visual clues they receive from other characters. Play around with those assumptions. Don't let your character always guess correctly. That's boring. Don't be boring.

Loving, Touching, Kissing

Love scenes are action scenes loaded with all of the descriptive tools we've been discussing—character's past, show vs. tell, deep POV, the five senses, visceral reactions, emotions, physical descriptions, and assumptions. Really this whole book has funneled us to this point. There is no greater joy than falling in love and expressing that love in a meaningful physical interaction.

From **The Opportunist** by Tarryn Fisher:

A few more feathery, light kisses and then he comes at me full force. Our mouths crush together like two angry thunderclouds.

From **Dark Wild Night** by Christina Lauren:

I never want to run out of clothes because every time he peels something away, he kisses me lower, hums against the skin, and bites just the smallest bit. It's like having lust uncorked and poured in bubbly streams across my skin.

From **The Opportunist** by Tarryn Fisher:

He is frozen; his whole body tense. I kiss him and try to melt away his resistance. It works and he comes at me like a flood. He breaks away from my lips to peel off his shirt and then he comes back so quickly I barely have time to breathe.

From **How to Misbehave** by Ruthie Knox:

Soft. His mouth was soft. His breath fanned over her face, and one of his hands came up and held the back of her head, mobbing it and tilting it just so. A new angle. A different kiss.

From **Arsen** by Mia Asher:

Ben grabs fistfuls of my hair in his hands and pulls me down for a kiss. A fiery kiss that blazes through me, burning me from the inside out. Ashes. His kiss turns me into ashes.

We won't get into love scenes...that's a *different* kind of workshop. But I want you to think about the emotional impact of love scenes and how the tone and tenor changes throughout your book as the lovers grow closer, as they fall in love. Love scene #1 will have a different feel and emotional impact than the last love scene of your book. Love scenes are a great way to show the progression of the relationship and you can show that through description. The early scenes will be more about the physical whereas the later sex scenes will be more about the emotional. Choose words that show that to your reader.

If you're going to write sex scenes don't cheat your reader out of the experience. The reader will know if you're not comfortable writing them. So if you have to look away from the screen as you type while praying no one ever reads what you're writing, then my advice to you is—DO NOT WRITE SEX SCENES. Just don't. There are other ways you can show sexual attraction without taking anybody's clothes off.

Love is confusing and exciting and frustrating and wonderful. Have fun with your love scenes. Be inventive and creative. This is not the time to turn your novel into an instruction manual—tab a into slot b. Bring everything you've learned in this book to your love scenes whether you close the door or keep it wide open.

In Closing...

Oh, no! We've come to the end of the book. I hope I've helped to open your mind to everything description can be and how you can make it work hard for you in your novel. If you enjoyed the excerpts I used as examples throughout the book I hope you'll consider reading them whether you check them out from your local library or buy them in ebook or print.

I thank you for making it this far in the book. If you enjoyed *Making Description Work Hard For You* I hope you'll consider leaving a review. Oh, what the heck. Leave a review even if you didn't enjoy the book. Reviews help authors so leave one whenever you can. It's a good habit to get into like flossing your teeth and making sure the refrigerator door's closed.

Before you go I have a little exercise for you to try your hand at. Remember that four sentence scene earlier in the book and how it was written two different ways? I want you to try your hand with the scene below. Using description, rewrite this scene:

Exercise:

She handed him a box with a bow. A present. She'd given him a gift and he had nothing for her.

"Open it," she said.

He did. "It's... Thank you."

A couple of things to think about—does your character like getting presents? Does the character like the person giving him or her the present? Does he like the gift? Feel free to change the sex of the characters to fit your scene.

If you remember nothing else from this book, remember this:

You, the author, are not doing the describing in a novel...*your characters are*.

Now go, be descriptive. AND DON'T BE ORDINARY.

Bibliography

Rush by Beth Yarnall
Copyright © 2012 Elizabeth Yarnall

Lush by Beth Yarnall
Copyright © 2014 Elizabeth Yarnall

A Deep and Dark December by Beth Yarnall
Copyright © 2015 Elizabeth Yarnall

Vindicate by Beth Yarnall
Copyright © 2015 Elizabeth Yarnall
Published by Loveswept, an imprint of Random
House, a division of Penguin Random House
LLC, New York, NY

Atone by Beth Yarnall
Copyright © 2016 Elizabeth Yarnall
Published by Loveswept, an imprint of Random
House Publishing Group, a division of Penguin
Random House LLC, New York, NY

Tempting a Proper Lady by Debra Mullins
Copyright © 2010 Debra Welch
Published by Avon Books, an imprint of Harper
Collins Publishers, LLC, New York, NY

Angelfall by Susan Ee
Copyright © 2011 Feral Dream, LLC

Dark Wild Night by Christina Lauren
Copyright © 2015 Christina Hobbs and Lauren
Billings
Published by Gallery Books, an imprint of
Simon & Schuster, Inc., New York, NY

Arsen by Mia Asher
Copyright © 2013 Mia Asher

The Opportunist by Tarryn Fisher
Copyright © 2012 Tarryn Fisher

Dirty Red by Tarryn Fisher
Copyright © 2012 Tarryn Fisher

Hot Head by Damon Suede
Copyright © 2011 Damon Suede
Published by Dreamspinner Press, Frisco, TX

About the Author

Best-selling author, Beth Yarnall, writes mysteries, romantic suspense, and the occasional hilarious tweet. A storyteller since her playground days, Beth remembers her friends asking her to make up stories of how the person `died' in the slumber party game Light as a Feather, Stiff as a Board, so it's little wonder she prefers writing stories in which people meet unfortunate ends. In middle school she discovered romance novels, which inspired her to write a spoof of soap operas for the school's newspaper. She hasn't stopped writing since.

For a number of years, Beth made her living as a hairstylist and makeup artist and even owned a salon. Somehow hairstylists and salons seem to find their way into her stories. Beth lives in Southern California with her husband, two sons, and their rescue dog where she is hard at work on her next novel.

For more information about Beth and her novels please visit her website:
www.bethyarnall.com

───────────●───────────

To stay up to date on the latest Beth Yarnall happenings, including new releases, sales, special announcements, exclusive excerpts, and giveaways, subscribe to my newsletter at:
www.bethyarnall.com

Printed in Great Britain
by Amazon